HCC Devotions

Revised For Our Changes

Mary Pollard Bethea

ARPress

ILLUMINATING IDEAS
EMPOWERING VOICES

ARPress
45 Dan Road Suite 5
Canton MA 02021
Hotline: 1(888) 821-0229
Fax: 1(508) 545-7580

Ordering Information:
Quantity sales. Special discounts are available on quantity purchases by corporations, associations, and others. For details, contact the publisher at the address above.

Printed in the United States of America.

| ISBN-13: | Softcover | 979-8-89389-561-2 |
| | eBook | 979-8-89389-562-9 |

Library of Congress Control Number: 2019920139

CONTENTS

Preface 1

About The Author 3

Opening prayer 4

Introduction Part 1 Better Prayers for Better Faith Life 7

Ailments 9

Anger 12

Anxiety 15

Bondage 18

Complaining 21

Doubt 24

A Better Life From Better Prayers . Part 2 Introduction 27

Encouragement 31

FAITH by Mary Bethea 34

Forgiveness 41

Godliness 43

Judgement 45

Kingdom Building 48

Liberty 50

Miracles 52

Upward Bound 54

Preface

"Finally, our brothers and sisters, pray for us, that the Lord's message may continue to spread rapidly and be received with honor, just as it was among you. Pray also, that God will rescue us from wicked and evil people; for not everyone believes the message. But the Lord is faithful, and He will strengthen you and keep you safe f r on the evil one." 2 Thessalonians 3:1-3 GNB

HELLO READERS OF the word of God. May you rejoice in the Lord always for the ability to walk and to talk with Jesus Christ, our Lord! This book, HCC Revised Devotions For Our Changes, seeks to better your relationship with your Creator. Each prayer, from beginning to end, will address exaltation and dedication as your way of life in Christ. Let God tell you how to overcome every trial and every victory. What's the difference from these prayers and the first book of HCC Devotions? These prayers are filled with wisdom and understanding that has come from the word of God. Prayer gets better and better from God's word that's hidden in your heart changing to manifestations of the Spirit. Let the anointing open your heart as you pray these prayers. Then, see how using unknown tongues will change your spiritual thoughts to spiritual things. Prayer betters your living once you compare spiritual things around you and things influencing you into actions for your good. Let the presence of the Lord bring salvation, healing, and deliverance. Cry out to the Lord daily! Bless His Holy Name! Come to Him with joy, with peace, with happiness!

For the Lord is Great and greatly to be praised! Amen. This book will shift your prayer atmosphere once you are friendly and accept His presence as a meek and humble servant! Prayer will never ever lose its power! Better your home! Better your church! Better your nation! We know now that it's not by might, nor by power, but by the Holy Spirit! Amen. Get better with God when you get better in prayer! Amen. Father God, this book is Yours for the uplifting of our hearts, souls, and minds as we walk in the Holy Spirit! Let every reader touch and agree that spiritual living will increase as our prayers increase in the word. We declare victory in every word that proceeds our of us from the gospel. We are not ashamed of this prayer life of faith, hope, and charity! Be blessed in the name of Jesus Christ, Amen and Amen.

About The Author

MARY POLLARD BETHEA is an ordained prayer warrior and missionary in her local church, Highway Christian Church of Gaithersburg, Maryland. She has written several devotional books, using this book as a revised edition. She holds a degree in Sociology and certificates in discipleship. Sister Mary was born in Washington, DC where she was raised by her parents, Bishop James L. and Missionary Dolly M Pollard. She is married and the mother of five children, the grandmother of twelve. To God be the glory for the wonderful things He has done. She continues to lead others to salvation and deliverance as a missionary in the Bible Way Church of Our Lord Jesus Christ. May God bless every member of the body of Christ as we build God's Kingdom on earth as it is in heaven. Be blessed in Your work for the Lord, in Jesus name. Amen and Amen.

Opening prayer

FATHER GOD BETTERS us and his špirit in us betters the lives of OTHERS

Father god in heaven, i thank you for your anointing over my life as i present YOUR book of anointed prayers, called the revised edition of HCC DEVOTIONS for change. This is a book to better our prayers as we choose to diligently seek you. Bless the lord, o my SOul! And all that is within me! Bless your holy name! Amen. Father, i pray TOday and every day for your blessings over these prayers to save souls! I pray for a better spiritual life so i can reveal your power and purpose in my HEART! Lord, let these prayers change many minds to better your kingdom on earth! life in christ gets better through the word of God being spoken and manifested on earth for your glory! Lord, let all my thoughts and prayers bring forth your salvation, healing, and deliverance that your will be doNE on earth as it is in heaven! Amen. Father God, i see a better life of spiritual blessings through this book! I pray for better wisdom, an increase in compassion, a shift in positions, and grace to abound, Exceedingly and abundantly, to all who acknowledge you in these prayers, o lord! Every word in the revised edition of HCC DEVOTIONS for change are devoted to you, almighty God. Master of the universe. i cleanse my heart in forgiveness To those who stand in the need of prayer. Blessed savior, i release YOur healing virtue to the hearers and doers of the word of god. We cry out holy! Holy! Holy! Lord, god almighty! Let the words of my mouth, and the meditation of my heart be acceptable in your SIGHt, O lord, my strength and my redeemer! These and all the blessing I ask in Jesus name. My prayers are here to bless others until that glorious day we see you face to face. Amen and amen.

Introduction
Part 1
Better Prayers
for Better Faith Life

"Come close to God and God will come close to You. Wash your hands, you sinners; purify your hearts for your loyalty is divided between God and the world. Let there be tears for what you have done! James4:8 NLT

Eternal God, Master of this universe, we come before You to give You glory and to give You praise! Father God, hear our cry today as we stand in the need of Your prayer, Your intercession. Bless the Lord, O my soul, and all that's within me. Bless Your Holy Name! Lord God, these prayers written by Missionary Mary are anointed and appointed to open the eyes of Your people. We seek the Kingdom of God and Your righteousness so better prayers will be added. Amen. Draw us near Lord as we pray in unknown tongues. Restore Your Spirit of love and compassion that conquers all! Lead us to walk better by faith, not by sight! We speak to that mountain of deceitfulness, every imagination that comes against the knowledge of You, our Lord and Savior! Increase our faith, Father God, as we depend on Your saving grace. Father God we wash our hands as forgivers to trespassers. Open our eyes, Lord Jesus, as You cleans us from all unrighteousness, all these strongholds that So easily beset us. Father God, bring salvation to the hearts and souls of every reader of these prayers. Father God, we rebuke the demons of idolatry, rebellion, and spiritual wickedness in high places, in the name of Jesus! Let every prayer in this book bring fruit to our spirit man and hope to our eternal rest. Lord, You are worth to be praised as the author and finished of our faith. Every stronghold: such as ailments, anger, anxiety, bondage, complaining, doubt and confusion, along with fear and rejection, we bind in the name of Jesus Christ! Let the redeemed of the Lord say so! Father we stand in blessed assurance that you will deliver us from all evil, in the name of Jesus! The just shall live by faith! Amen. Thank You, Lord God, from whom all blessings flow! Thank You, Lord, for planting Your seed of righteousness in our hearts, our souls, and our minds. Father, we call You "Abba" our Father who has adopted us to establish Your Kingdom on earth. Let Your will be done in our lives. We will forever honor You Lord and give You all the praise! On Jesus name we pray, Amen and Amen.

Ailments

"Many are the afflictions of the righteous, but the Lord delivers him out of them all!" Psalms 34:19 NKJV.

FATHER GOD IN heaven, You are our Alpha and Omega, our beginning and our ending of life. This is our prayer of faith for the healing of our ailments, our afflictions. We pray, Father God, to You, Jehovah Rapha, our God who heals. Your word says that the righteous faces many troubles, trials and tribulations. You have spoken these words and they heal us. Father God, we speak Your word that says, "Blessed are those who are persecuted for righteousness' sake, for theirs is the Kingdom of heaven." Matthew 5:10 We thank You, Father for these blessings due to persecution. Lord, we praise You for Your blessed assurance that great is our reward. Lord, You bless us for doing the right things even when we are mocked, lied on, and mistreated as believers. NLT says in Matthew 5:12, "Be happy about it! Be very glad! For a great reward awaits you in heaven! Remember that the ancient prophets were persecuted the same way!" Father, we know that we work while it is day to magnify and glorify You, Ancient One! "But You, Jesus, was wounded for our transgressions, You, Lord, was bruised for our inequities; the chastisement for our peace was upon You, and by Your stripes we are healed!" We pray night and day, Lord, in the name of Jesus, that our joy will be full and pleasing in Your sight, O Lord. Father, Your word says, "Do not fear any of those things which you are about to suffer...Be faithful until death and I will give you the crown of life!" Revelations 2:10 NKJV Almighty God! You remind us that the sufferings of this present time are not worthy to be compared with the glory which shall be revealed in us. Our minds are changing from faith to faith into wisdom and overpowering love which is the mind of Christ! Glory to You, God Almighty! You have spoken that You will deliver us out of all of our troubles, out of all of our ailments and pains. You are our present help in the time of trouble! Prophet Isaiah preached Your word for us to listen and speak into our hearts! NLT of Isaiah 53 says, " Yet it was our weaknesses Christ carried; it was our sorrows that weighed Him down. We thought His troubles were a punishment from God…He was beaten so we could be whole. He was whipped so we could be healed!" Amen! We praise You, Jesus our Savior, for shedding Your blood for our salvation that washes away all our sins. Jesus, You manifested all sin as an affliction, a sickness or disease. You say, Father of Heaven and earth, that the Lord laid on You the sins of us all. Why, Lord! Father we cry out to You knowing that all of us, like sheep have strayed away from the Lord at some time or another. We all have rebelled to follow our own paths. But God! Lord only You can heal us, deliver us from evil in the name of Jesus! Our Creator! Father You say to us, "Fear not! I will never leave you or forsake you"! We have to speak boldly as You have spoken to us, " The Lord is my light and my salvation, whom shall I fear. You, Lord, is the strength of my life, of whom shall I be afraid!" Amen. Lord, we have no good thing dwelling in our flesh! We cry out to You, Lord! We hear Your answer saying, "Come to Me all of you who are weary and carry heavy burdens, and I will give You rest! Take My yoke upon you". Victory is in You, Christ Jesus, our Savior! We give You all the glory and all the praise, in the precious name of Jesus for our deliverance. Thank You, Lord for saving our souls, thank You, Lord for making us whole. We cry out to You, Lord, "Our times are in Your hand, Lord; Deliver us from the hands of our enemies, and from those who persecute us. Make Your face shine upon Your servant, in the name of Jesus! Father God, You are a lamp into our feet and a light to our pathways. Your word, Lord, removes all evil afflictions to renew our hearts, our souls, and our minds in Christ Jesus! Lord, we put away our sinful earthly thoughts and emotions to be transformed by the renewing of our minds! We are Holy! Lord, it's Your will for us to be made holy! We present ourselves as living sacrifices, holy, acceptable to You, Lord, which is our reasonable service. Amen. You have called us, Lord, to heal the sick, raise the dead, cleanse the lepers, and cast out demons. Lord, what we freely have received from You teaches us that we are here to freely bless others and better their lives in Christ! We trust You Lord! We have no confidence in humans! We cry out to You, Father of Your Holy Kingdom, "We shall no die but live" from ailments, sickness and diseases, for Your glory. We declare the works of the Lord to better us! This is the day the Lord has made, we will rejoice and be glad in it! Hallelujah! Glory to God! We are delivered from all ailments, all heartaches and pains! In Jesus name we pray for the salvation and healing of others who look to Christ, our Savior! Amen and Amen!

Anger

"Be angry(at sin-at immorality, at injustice, at ungodly behavior), yet do not sin; do not let your anger (cause you shame, nor allow it) to last until the sun goes down." Ephesians 4:26 AMPL

FATHER GOD IN heaven, we love You with all our heart, all our soul, and all our mind. We adore You, our Father, for the gift of the Holy Spirit that keeps our mouths from speaking guile. Father God, You have blessed us to understand how anger, that feeling of flared temper, may cause harm to our hearts, our souls, and our minds. We will Bless the Lord at all times and Your praises shall continually be in our mouths! Amen. Lord, we thank You for Your word teaching us to show the world that we do get angry or upset over immorality and injustices. "A gentle answer deflects anger, but harsh words make tempers flare." Proverbs 15:1 We speak life into ourselves and to others to keep harsh words from causing harm. Father God, we pray Your word without ceasing to deflect anger, those evil thoughts and actions. We regard no one according to the flesh Father God. "Now all things are of You, God, and You have reconciled us to You through Jesus Christ!" 2 Corinthians 5:18 says, "Let the words of our mouths and the meditations of our hearts be acceptable in your sight, O Lord, our strength and Redeemer." Father God, Jehovah Tsidkenu, our Righteousness! We pray for Your will to be done in our ministry, in every prayer we speak to stop the power of the enemy. Father, in the name of Jesus, we ask for a double portion of Your fruit! Let not our hearts be troubled when we speak against immorality and injustice! Lord, we know Your words will heal and deliver souls! Anger will be deflected in our thoughts of anger so truth and kindness can be revealed. We pray this prayer of faith to remove hardness so the fruit of the Spirit can prevail. Create in us a clean heart and renew Your righteousness before the sun goes down. Father God we bless You for taking away all our sin, all our anger and evil deeds with Your cleansing blood! Amen. We no longer follow the desires of the flesh! We have been crucified from the flesh acts and thoughts! Amen. You word says, "Get rid of bitterness, rage, anger, harsh words, and slander, as well as all types of evil behavior." Father Your word explains to us that anger brings judgement, facing hellfire. We receive Your word as we pray and understand that anger can be quick, causing us to sin! Human anger! Anger can be sin in our hearts and minds, but Your word, Lord, causes us to speak with the fruit of self control, love, peace, kindness, all gentleness, and longsuffering. Spirit filled when anger is chilled! Father in heaven, teach us Your ways of control so we are obedient to Your will! Father God, it is for Your glory that we lift up the name of Jesus to cause no shame on Your word, no space for unbelief in our thoughts and works for Christ. Lord we speak boldly in the name of Jesus that we repent! We turn from being angry and disrespectful! We trust and obey Your word, Father, according to Proverbs that tells us to have godly understanding to control our anger so hot tempers will stop along with evildoings and great foolishness. Thank You, Father for leading our path by telling us to pursue righteousness and Your unfailing love and mercy, then we will receive eternal life and honor with Your righteousness. Amen. Hallelujah! Lord, we bless You for Your teaching in Ecclesiastes 7:9, saying how anger labels us as fools! Lord, let us be sensible, showing the goodness of Jesus and how Your mercy endures forever. We understand You have forgiven us just as we forgive others by overlooking their wrongs! Glory to God in the highest for our deliverance from the strongholds of anger and rage, in Jesus name we pray. Amen and Amen.

Want to insert a picture from your files or add a shape or text box? You got it! On the Insert tab of the ribbon, just tap the option you need.

Anxiety

We are humans, but we do not wage war as humans do. We use God's mighty weapons, not worldly weapons; to knock down the strongholds of human reasoning and to destroy false arguments. We destroy every proud obstacle that keeps people from knowing God! We capture their rebellious thoughts and teach them to obey Christ! 2 Corinthians 10:3-5 NLT

PRAISE YOU JEHOVAH! Our Almighty God of this world and the world to come! Father God, You are our Creator and our Substainer! Thank You Father, You are our Jehovah Jireh, our Provider! Hallelujah! We give You thanks in all things, for only You, God, gives us life, health, and strength. Our prayer is for Your overcoming power to increase in us as we face anxieties, those situations of emotional instabilities. We pray like Job, saying, Lord! How frail is humanity and how short is life!? We know, Father God, how to speak Your word and say, I can do all things through Christ who strengthens me! Lord, hear our cry as we turn over all our misery and confusion into Your hands. The human stronghold of anxiety can only be destroyed when we speak Your word, removing those human reasonings and emotional setbacks. We hear you saying, '„Come to Me all of you who are weary and carry heavy burdens, and I will give you rest!' Great is Your faithfulness! We praise You, Lord, in every situation knowing how to give thanks in everything. Christ, our Lord, You have rescued us from the curse of the law, thoughts on fleshly emotions and insecurities. Father God, we walk by faith now and forevermore, not by sight. We pray your word to strengthen our spiritual thoughts to be obedient to Christ. 'Love never gives up, never loses faith, is always hopeful, and endures through every circumstance." Lord, My God, You will work it out in our warfare. Father, we know that our weapons of the Holy Spirit are mighty because we trust and believe You will deliver us out of every anxiety attack. Father God, in the name of Jesus, we will worship You as we put on the whole armor of God to resist the enemy. Yes God, we stand on Your word putting on the belt of truth, wearing Your breastplate of righteousness in our hearts, praying in Your Spirit of unknown tongues for revelation and deliverance! Father, we fight the good fight of faith by asking You Lord to help us overcome, to keep us, knowing You will carry us through. Almighty God! We cleanse our hearts, our minds and souls with forgiveness and love for one another. It's Christ who lives in us, We live, we move, and we have our being! We say Yes to You Lord who brings us out! You've done great things! Great things! Father God, to You be all the glory for giving us shoes of peacemakers to share Your word, not human thoughts. Thank You Father for the written and Spoken word, our shield of faith, our Holy Spirit inside of us, which is salvation, and our sword that we speak using Your Word in all occasions. We pray, Father God, that we release Your power. Christ, we pray for Your mind, sound and strong, be spoken as we fight anxieties and other forces of evil in the atmosphere. We stand for power and love, not the forces of darkness, evil rulers of the unseen world, and spiritual wickedness moving in heavenly places. Love overcomes all evil! Whom the Son has set free is free indeed from fears, all anxieties and tricks of the enemy. Amen! Praise You, O Lord! Philippians chapter three teaches us to be overcomers by focusing on praising and worshiping Christ Jesus for Your death of the human flesh that is victory in the Holy Spirit! Amen. We are forgetting those things behind us, in the name of Jesus, every act and ungodly thought that we suffer in the flesh! We sing, 'Shake, Shake, Shake! Shake the devil off! Shake, shake, shake! Shake the devil off! Shout! Shout! Shout! Bless the name of Jesus! Shout! Shout! Shout! Bless His Holy Name! We thank and praise You, Father, for Your mighty weapons You have provided! You have delivered from the hands of the enemy. We declare victory over the stronghold of anxieties and fear! The word has set us free! The day is now when true worshipers will worship You in Spirit and in truth! No weapon turned against us will succeed. We will silence every voice raised up to accuse us. These are benefits Father, Your servants enjoy. You have spoken, in Jesus name, Amen. Father we honor our Savior for being the same yesterday, today, and forevermore. You send Your word, and it always produces fruit. It always accomplishes all and prospers all where it is sent. Amen. My God is an awesome God! Awesome wisdom, power, and love He gives us from heaven above! Keep us Father, in Your eternal mind of Christ! We pray for the body of Christ, the lost to come to the knowledge of You, and the future generations to follow Christ. You are the Keeper of life, our salvation! Let the words of our mouths, and the meditation of our hearts be acceptable in Your sight, O Lord, our strength and Redeemer. In Jesus name we pray, Amen and Amen.

Bondage

"Do not let sin control the way you live; do not give in to sinful desires. Do not let any part of your body become an instrument of evil to serve sin. Instead, give yourselves completely to God, for you were dead, but now you have new life. So use your whole body as an instrument to do what is right for the glory of God. Sin is no longer your master...Instead you live under the freedom of God's grace. You can be a slave to sin, which leads to death, or you can choose to obey God, which leads to righteous... living." Romans 6:12-16 NLT

HEAVENLY FATHER, WE worship You as our Lord and Savior of this world. Father, We give You praise for all You plant in us to grow for Your glory. Thank You, Lord, today for this prayer time in the midst of problems and pains. We know Lord, that only You can give us Your peace in the midst of every storm. Father God, we ask You to increase our faith. Deliver us, Lord, from the traps of the enemy. This prayer to set us free from the strongholds of bondage is possible only if we believe Father, that You are willing and able to show us! All things are possible if we only believe! This prayer is preparing us for the good fight we face to remove strongholds and every weight of bondage. Deliver us from every weight that so easily has overtaken our peace Lord God! Why should we be bound when You, our Father, has set us free? You are the keeper of our life. Father, We are free from every stronghold that we have faith and believe is under our feet! We have to walk in faith and not in fear! Strongholds are evil and sinful ways! Let God arise and the enemy be scattered! Father God, in the name of Jesus, we rebuke that rebellious spirit of captivity! We cast all doubts of God's Holy power into the pit of hell! Father let this same Jesus who was crucified be revealed in our minds and souls as God of victory and God of all strength! Our Lord and Redeemer! Hallelujah! Thank You, Jesus! Father God, You sent Your Son to earth from heaven that Your glory be revealed to Your footstool. Jesus wore the body like sinners on earth and in that body Father, You declared an end to sin's control! You, Father, ended the control of the enemy by sacrificing Your Son for our sins! Amen. Whom the Son has set free is free indeed! No more doubts, no more losses, no more failures or faults! We are free, no longer bound by sin and death! We are free of guilt and innocent of all sins! Amen. Today and everyday we have Father God, Your righteousness, to bind whatever on earth and it will be bound in heaven. We bind those evil spirits of unbelief in the power of Jesus. We bind idolatry and evil speaking, envy, strife, and jealousy in the name of Jesus! Whatever we loose on earth will be loosed in heaven. Father God we loose a double portion of Your favor, Your increase in our love for one another, and power to discern the will of God. Amen. We stand with power and authority over all devils through Jesus Christ! Now is the time for all God's people to lift up Holy hands! Lift up Holy hearts! Lift up Holy minds! Lift up Holy souls in the name of Jesus Christ our Lord! Hallelujah! Praise Your Holy name! Let us run the race of grace that is set before us! Amen. We live in the freedom of God's grace. We present our bodies, Father God, as living sacrifices like Christ Jesus! We are holy and acceptable to You, Lord, which is our reasonable service! We are not conformed to this world but we are transformed by the renewing of our minds from faith to faith. Father, we are a new creation, forgetting things behind us! All things have become new! Since we are surrounded by such a huge crowd of witnesses, let us run this race into eternity knowing we are changed for better living and better giving of our newness daily! Let God be true and every man be a liar! Nothing but the blood of Jesus can make us whole again. Amen. Lord, Jehovah Tsidkenu, our Righteousness, we bless You for our salvation and the blood that keeps us from day to day. Father, You teach us to speak to that mountain, that stronghold of sin, that keeps us bound to our mistakes and fears. Father, we speak to those things in the name of Jesus! We submit ourselves to Your mighty hand for discipline in Your word.. We keep our eyes focused on the author and finisher of our faith. Let Your peace abound in our hearts, minds, and souls. Father, let Your will be done on earth as it is in heaven. Thank You Father for these and all the blessings in Jesus name, Amen and Amen.

Complaining

"Do all things without complaining and disputing, that you may become blameless and harmless children of God, without fault in the midst of a crooked and perverse generation, among whom you shine as lights in the world." Philippians 2:14-15 NKJV

PRECIOUS LORD! WE lift up the name of Jesus! Our prayer today and everyday is to build our hope in Christ! Father God, break those strongholds of complaining and disputing, the work of the enemy attacking our hope and peace! You are the Alpha and Omega! Our hope is built on You to give us Your revelation knowledge! Give us Lord Jesus, Your wisdom that passes all understanding! Cleanse us Lord with Your word as we forgive our neighbors, take away those strongholds of dissatisfaction and resentment. Amen. Father, Your word says those who are still under the control of their sinful nature can never please You! Strengthen us right now Lord Jesus, to please You by repenting and forgiving, by acknowledging You in all our ways. Amen. We pray for Your blood to control us! The blood of Jesus has forgiven us as we forgive others, both friends and foes. Hear our prayers, O Lord! Examine us, O Lord, and prove us. Try our mind and our heart…We have walked in Your truth! Amen. We pray that our hearts burn within us like the scripture in Luke 24:32 as the Holy Spirit talks to us on this journey to meet You, Lord Jesus. Father, Father, up in heaven, we go to You in prayer knowing You give us life, and life more abundantly. We pray Psalms 26 saying to You, Lord help us. We bind the enemy of complaining by depending on Your word, "We trust in You, Lord and we shall not slip!" We declare that we are blameless and harmless children of God by speaking the word of God! We wash our hands in innocense, O Lord, that we may proclaim Your glory! Lord, God, we sing with the voices of thanksgiving of Your wondrous works! No weapon formed against us shall prosper, in the name of Jesus! Thank You, Lord for delivering us from the hands of the enemy! We will bless the Lord at all times, Your praises shall continually be in our mouth. We sought You, Lord, and You heard us. Amen. Thank You, Father, for removing the strongholds of fear and complaining, the evil spirits of rebellion and bitterness. We do not judge others from this day forward knowing how we will be condemned for condemning others. We speak Your truths, God that You have not given us a spirit of complaining out of fear. You have given us Your Holy Spirit of power. Love and a sound mind are spoken by Your children, Lord, to give us power and authority to cast out devils, in the name of Jesus, Amen and Amen. We are not ashamed of the gospel of Jesus Christ that teaches us to pray without ceasing for the lost, for daily bread, as we take up our cross to follow Christ. We shine as lights on a hill that cannot be hidden. We shine as lights in this perverse and crooked generation. Let the redeemed of the Lord say so. Father God, thank you for healing our hearts, our minds, and our souls from the stronghold that causes our thoughts and words to be about complaining. Romans the eighth chapter teaches us Christ lives in us even though our bodies have sin. "The Spirit gives us life because we have been made right with God. The Holy Spirit has set us free from complaining, sin and death. Amen. Bless the Lord, O my soul, bless Your holy name. We speak victory over that spirit of complaining and disputing as we speak to ourselves saying, "There is therefore now no condemnation to those who are in Christ Jesus, who do not walk according to the flesh, but according to the Spirit!" We trust and believe, Father God who has created a workmanship in us, to save us, to heal us, and to deliver us from all sin and shame. We won't complain! In the precious name of Jesus we pray one for another, Amen and Amen.

Doubt

"But let him ask in faith, with no doubting, for he who doubts is like a wave of the sea driven and tossed by the wind." James 1:6 NKJV

FATHER GOD UP in heaven, send Your glory to those praying earnestly for Your answer, Your power to deliver. God of all nations and heavens, we bless Your holy name! Speak to our hearts, Lord, as we forgive our sisters and brothers, even the unforgiveable, in the precious name of Jesus! Let us not waver or doubt Your power, Lord, as we come before You in prayer and intercession. Father God, there is a balm in Gilead to heal a sin sick soul! Hallelujah! Our prayers are for deliverance in our souls as we cast out the demons and evil spirits that so easily attack our minds and actions, in the name of Jesus! O the blood of Jesus that washes us white as snow when we let go of every weight of doubt. Father God, we speak what You tell us in 2 Corinthians 3:16-17, "Nevertheless, when we turn to You, Lord, the veil is taken away. Now, Lord, You are The Spirit and where the Spirit of the Lord is, there is liberty! Thank You, Lord, for these comforting words to sooth us and heal us from every doubt in our minds and souls. Thank You Lord, for ripping that veil of unbelief, that veil of uncertainty and denial as Your ambassador! We are Your disciples who are ordained, like the prophets of old, to spread the Good News!

You speak into our hearts, saying, "Go into all the world and preach the gospel to every creature. He who believes and is baptized will be saved; but he who does not believe will be condemned." Thank You, Lord, for keeping us living by Your word and our testimonies. We count it all joy to go through many tests, to stand when all others fail. We rejoice in You, Lord always and serve You with gladness. We obey Your word that says ask and it shall be given. We know whatever we ask in Your name, Jesus Christ, believing, we will receive. We read in John chapter one that You came to earth to set us free from unbelief, from death. All who believe You and accept You as Lord and Savior, Father God, You give us the right to become children of God! We pray that all doubt be removed from Your children, that they call on the name of Jesus to reveal faith in God. Your word reveals how uncertainty leads to death, a double minded man who is unstable in all his ways. Thank You Lord, for revealing how doubt has to be cast out of our minds and souls because it comes up against the knowledge and power of God in us. Let us speak the word of God in us, the wisdom You have planted in us to deliver us from the strongholds of the enemy. Amen. We cry out Holy! Holy! Lord God Almighty! God has raised us up from our death in sin to a new creation in Christ. We pray and intercede in tongues of the Holy Spirit for those who are weak in the faith. Romans 14:1 we are told, Lord, to receive one who is weak in the faith but not to dispute over things in doubt. Father, You are not pleased with doubt and unbelief. We speak 2 Corinthians 2:5 saying, pray "that our faith should not be in the wisdom of men but in the power of God." We pray for our government, our US leaders in the White House, the Congress, the Courts, and the Cabinet, that the God of peace will crush satan under our feet as we say grace and peace be magnified! O Lord our Savior. Mark 11:22_23 Jesus speaks to us, saying, "Have faith in

God. For assuredly I say to you, whoever says to this mountain, 'Be removed and be cast into the sea, and does not doubt in your heart, but believes those things you say will be done, you will have whatever you say." Amen. Thank. You Jesus. Thank You Lord! Jesus is Lord! We ask now and forever in faith with no doubt that God will bring us out on time! In Jesus name we pray, Amen and Amen.

A Better Life
From Better Prayers .
Part 2
Introduction

Bless the Lord, O our souls and all that is within us, Bless Your Holy name! For You have done great things for us. Eternal God our Father, there is none like You! Father God, we praise and exalt your name as we minister in prayer. We speak to the Holy Spirit inside of us to lead and guide us as Your children. Our souls make a boast in You, O Lord for the humble to hear us and be glad! O magnify the Lord with us, all of our readers and believers in Christ! We are here for such a time as this to exalt Your name together! Hallelujah! Amen! Father, we praise You today and everyday for being a Wonderful Counselor! Our Mighty God! Our Everlasting Father! Our Prince of Peace! Hallelujah! Hallelujah! Only You, Lord, know all hearts and what the Spirit is saying to us right now! Father, let Your Holy Spirit in us reveal what You are pleading to Your believers! Hallelujah! We pray today, Father, that we will be obedient and be in harmony with Your will! We seek answers, Father, to better receive the laws You have placed in our hearts! Give us a double portion of Your anointing now, Father, as we open our minds to Your cleansing power and Your saving grace! There is power in the name of Jesus to make yokes easy and our burdens light! Hallelujah! You have given us Your Son, that Holy power from heaven, to walk by faith as Your vessels! Father, we know how He shed His blood to cleanse us, to dissolve every sinful way in us! We are in Your gates of thanksgiving and praising You in heavenly places for giving us Your righteousness! Let Your glory rise among us, let Your blessings rise among us! Let Your increase rise among us! O' O' Lord! Let it rise! We pray for increase, Lord, in our mind of Christ, our wisdom! Increase our favor, O Lord, in our faith walk and our earthly teaching! Father, Your will be done as You shift us and show us the better side of life in Your presence of increase. Our hope, Father God, is built on nothing but Your blood and righteousness. We know, Father in heaven, that we have to fully trust in You with sincere hearts for Your living water to flow in us. Father, let that river of life overflow as we affirm Your power over all the power of the enemy! We speak life saying, "Our guilty consciences have been sprinkled with the blood of Jesus to make us clean, and out bodies have been washed with pure water." You say, Father, 'Except we are born of water and Spirit, we cannot enter the Kingdom of God!" So Your word, Father, and Your blood, and the Holy Spirit are One, full of living water, our river of life. We thank You, Father, for these three avenues of Your power and authority in us to save us, to heal us, and to prophesy over us as our deliverance from the hands of the enemy! Amen! Father, thank You for reminding us in the scripture, John 6:63, where You say, "The Spirit alone gives eternal life…and the very words I have spoken to you are Spirit and life!" Father, You see where unbelief lies in the hearts of many but You have come to give us life and life more abundantly. That's the better prayers from You we need as You intercede for us daily! We are one in the Spirit, one in the body of Christ! Amen. We pray for our cups to run over in Your grace and truth, Amen.

Encouragement

"Blessed be the Lord, because He has heard the voice of my supplications! The Lord is my strength and my shield; my heart trusted in Him, and I am helped. Therefore, my heart greatly rejoices. And with my song I will praise Him!"

WE PRAY THIS prayer of encouragement to our Everlasting Father, God of heaven and earth. Father God we bless You for all You have created in us to worship and glorify Your name. We thank You Father for faith, hope, and charity in everything we do and say. We praise Father God for hearing our supplications. Only You, Lord Jesus, knows what we should pray for because You have created us to serve and obey Your word. Our prayer, Lord, is to lift Your name up higher and higher for the world to see. Father, we know You are in heaven with the mighty power vested in Your people to draw all men to Your salvation. Let our prayers, Father God, lift the burdens and the cares of Your children. We pray for the lost to find Christ, for every prayer to avail much as we seek Your face. Create in us a clean heart, O Lord, and renew a right spirit of encouragement in us for one another. Father, Father, up in heaven! We come to You in prayer because we know that Your know that Your word is true. Father, You hear us, You will meet our petitions, and You will provide all our needs. You have given us Your power to obey Your word and to stay in Your will. Amen. We cry out to our brothers and sisters in the Lord, "Have you heard the counsel of God? Do you limit wisdom to yourselves?" No! No! We pray from Job

13:1 for better discernment as we encourage ourselves in the Lord by saying, "Behold, our eyes have seen all this. Our ears have understood it!" Father, we understand that when we come to You, we must believe that You are God and Father! You are Son of God and Holy Spirit! We must believe Lord, that You are a rewarder to those who diligently seek You. Every praise is to our God! Every word of worship on one accord! Every praise, every praise, is to our God! Hallelujah! We enter Your gates with thanksgiving and we enter Your courts with praise! We are thankful and bless Your Name! We are encouraged by Your word to ask and it shall be given, to seek and we shall find, to knock and the door will be opened. We suffer with You, Lord, all the day long. Now we know that we reign on earth with You as the Holy Spirit in the hearts of the body of Christ. Your covenant keeps us in agreement with Your word, Lord God. Father, You encourage us in the word to walk by faith and not by sight! You have revealed this to us who depend on Your word, "Truly, I tell you if two of you on earth agree about anything you ask for, it will be done by Father God in heaven. For where two or three gather in My name, there l am with them." So Lord, we know that without faith, we cannot see God. We encourage ourselves Lord, by saying scriptures, "Don't worry about anything, instead, pray about everything. Tell God what you need and thank You Lord for all You have done." Philippians 4:4 "I can do all things through Christ who strengthens me." "Father, You give power to the weak, and to those who have no might You increase strength!" Isaiah 40:29 If we wait on the Lord, we will renew our strength! If we trust in You, Lord, Your glory will be revealed in us. We have to encourage each other when we are weak by saying the things You have spoken, "Peace be still". Let us walk like You Jesus, talk like You, and tell others how You lead and guide us along the way everyday! Father we will not cast away our confidence which has great reward. Great is our reward in heaven. We are healed by the blood of the lamb, You our Father, and the words of our testimonies. The more we give of ourselves, the more we receive from giving! Thank You, Lord, for the gift of the Holy Spirit that allows us to acknowledge You, Lord, in all our ways, and lean not to our own understanding. Father God, we pray for our steps to be ordered by the Lord for Your delight in our ways. We pray to lay aside every weight as we look to You, Jesus, the author and finisher, of our faith! Lord we believe! Lord we will receive! Lord let Your word decree, in the name of Jesus! May You, Lord, bless and keep us. Lord, make Your face shine upon us, and be gracious to us. Lord, lift up Your countenance upon us and give us peace. In Jesus name we pray, Amen and Amen.

FAITH by Mary Bethea

I John 5:14-15 "Now this is the confidence we have in Him, that if we ask anything according to His will, He hears us. And if we know that He hears us, whatever we ask, we know that we have the petitions that we have asked Him."

BLESS MY FATHER, God of heaven and earth, from whom all blessings flow. God has established His believers to have faith that all things are possible if you trust and believe His Word. His people are called by His name and commanded to believe He will do what He said He would do. Our Father commands you to love Him first and believe in Him first, before you love yourself. This ability to believe before you receive, trust in Him first, is your faith. God wants your confidence in Him and not in what you see every day. You should know by now that the things you see and trust, such as your employer or your lawyer, are not to be trusted. Anything happens when you believe what others say and do. But God, when you read His Word and believe what He says will come to pass, then you know your confidence is established. Basically, God wants you to see that He has the power to keep you faithful and true to Him. Others will eventually let you down causing you to lose trust in them. When all others fail, God wants you to know you can stand on His promises. Isaiah 40:29-31 says, "He gives power to the weak, and to those who have no might He increases strength. Even the youths shall faint and be weary, and the young men shall utterly fall, but those who wait on the Lord shall renew their strength;

they shall mount up with wings like eagles, they shall run and not be weary. They shall walk and not faint." Now that the meaning of faith has been explained, you can build up your faith through things taught in the Word of God.

The faith chapter, Hebrews chapter 11, starts off with this scripture, "Now faith is the substance of things hoped for, the evidence of things not seen." Faith is substance, it's the Spirit in you, the part of you that is not of the flesh. God's definition of faith lets you see that you have to believe you can walk out of your flesh; say things that are not from your selfish speech but out of the supernatural; see things that you want to bring into your life before it happens; do things for others that you wouldn't ordinarily do; and hear things from God that no one else has spoken. Once you believe the way He wants you to, depending on Him to tell you everything, then you know how much faith you have in Him. Just ask yourself every time you make a decision, "Did I ask the Lord about it?", then you can see that you have to take your time to seek God's answer. Haste makes waste! Now you see that the quicker you talk to God, He is just as quick to answer you. God gives you power when you're weak. Once you build up your faith, the power to get a job by believing or to move into the house you prayed for, you still need strength from God to keep what you have asked from Him. Where is your faith when things happen that you did not ask from God? Do you have enough might to speak to the storm and say, "Peace be still!"? God will give you the strength if you are asking Him first what to do. God, in Isaiah 35:15, is saying, "Now is the time for all My people to humble themselves and pray and turn from their evil way of depending on another so I can get all the praise for bringing them out!" Faith will give you the strength to say, "I AM"! God wants you to see His salvation, even while you are weak. He declares that you will have your strength renewed, with strength like an eagle, strength to use His power higher than you can imagine. God knows you struggle and may fall from having strong faith, But God, He is with you when you wait on Him alone! God will give you the strength to run clear through things while others are struggling and strength to walk with clarity through problems without worry or distress. Isaiah 46:11-13 tells you what God will do for you, "Indeed I have spoken it; I will also bring it to pass. I have purposed it; I will also do it! Listen to me you stubborn hearted, My salvation shall not linger..." So all you need to do is believe. If things are not what you thought it would be, guess what, God gives you His salvation for it to be manifested whether you like it or not! You are in a win-Win situation where God has your back to deliver you and strengthen you if you will only trust Him! Trust Him! Trust Him! God Is! Let your spirit flow out of you to allow you to be confident that you will keep what God has given. Set your heart on God to get more blessings that are in store for you because whatever you ask the Father, in the name of Jesus, you shall receive! You are here to please God through praise and worship. Is that too hard for you to do? Tell everyone about the blessings God has provided to build your hope up on eternal life. The more you give others your testimony on how God keeps blessing you, the more your confidence grows, your God is great in good and bad times. This keeps you looking for things that will change your life today, tomorrow, and things that you hope will be forever in your life. God wants your faith to improve your life now and the lives of others in your family, in your community, in your state, in your country, and in this world. Why? Read Hebrews 11 and see what faith does when you work it.

Hebrews 10:35-38 lets you know why you use faith continually, you need to keep the strength God has given you so you won't lose it. "Do not cast away your confidence, which has great reward!" Faith keeps you ready for God's return to earth, He has promised to come back for you! "Now the just shall live by faith, not by sight, but by faith or your dependence on God alone to guide you. There is no time to look back on how you used to live, selfish and serving all kinds of gods, the one's in your family, your food, and your fun. Now, God lets you know that you have to trust in the Lord always, and lean not to your own understanding. You depended on Him to bless you in the supernatural arena. Now is the time for you show others your purpose, the things He has already made known for you to do in God's will. It's time to remove your fears, will I speak right or testify right. Let go and let God tell you how to talk. Prayer is the only answer because that's the time you tell God your needs. This is a short one while you're in the midst of a storm, "Father, I give all honor and praise to you today. I forgive those who cause harm to me, Lord. I ask, in Jesus name, that You forgive me for the things I do out of your will and show me what to do, what to say to obey your Word. Give me wisdom as I pray for my enemies, forgiving them who cause harm to Your body. I ask for revelation knowledge in my life for Your good, Lord. In Jesus name I pray, Amen." Once you declare and decree God's blessings over your life knowing that God will supply all of your needs, keep the faith. Each day has the simple question, "Lord, what shall I do for You today? Order my mouth, my hands, and my feet to be obedient to Your Word!" Look in Hebrews 11 and see how faith blessed Abraham's seed forever, faith made kings, faith made the weak strong yesterday, today, and forever. Jesus walked the earth to show you that faith can be like a grain, very, very small, to move huge barriers in your life. Once you allow that other body that moves out of you into the supernatural, leaving behind your doubts, fears, confusion, hurts, and pains, you can rely on faith. Break every stronghold in your heart to see the salvation of the Lord! God gives you a clean heart for keeps, not the one that's here today and gone tomorrow! He renews a right spirit in you daily when you ask Him. That's called depending on God, having faith to be the "Impossible You"! Can I do it? Yes, YOU Can! Lay aside every weight; every fear you can tell God to remove that's in your mind, your will, and your emotions. You are a treasure beyond measure! Now you can say Luke

9:23 with strong faith to others, "Then He said to them all, "If anyone desires to come after Me, let him deny himself, and take up His cross daily, and follow Me.'" God knows you can be all you want to be and some more, you are anointed and appointed for His purpose, to be like Him! What is that?

God prepares you first to do His will. He strengthens you to hold onto your faith, then He arms you for battle to win others to Christ. God says His kingdom will be done on earth as it is in heaven. How? He uses His people to establish the kingdom of God on earth. First, come to Jesus all who labor and are feeling heavy about it. He will give you wisdom to rest. The battles are not yours, they belong to the Lord. Galatians 5:10 lets you know that God has confidence in you to have no other mind but the mind of Christ, full of the fruits of the Spirit. Once you have developed faith, Jesus has prepared you to bear fruit. He gives you His fruit to give out to others; love, joy, peace, longsuffering, kindness, goodness, faithfulness, gentleness, and self-control. What is strength? Your dependence on God has given you His mind to walk by faith, not by sight. It has given you the will to ask God what can I do for You, not what are You going to do for me. Now God knows you should have your emotions put in His hands which are full of self- control. "There is therefore now no condemnation to those who are in Christ Jesus, who do not walk according to the flesh, but according to the Spirit." (Romans 8:1) Are you able to rest in Christ Jesus knowing you are walking in the Spirit? Yes. You can do what God wants you to do and go where He sends you, saying what He wants you to say. How can you do that? Ephesians 6:10 encourages you to be strong in the Lord and the power of His might. You are God's seed and He has planted other things inside of you once you deny yourself and bear your cross. He commands you to love Him, first, then He commands love for one another, second. Love covers a multitude of sin. God has given you fruit to fight sin and has prepared you to be a sanctuary. Once you devote your life to being in

His presence, full of worship, praise, prayer, the scriptures, and full of love from your church family who feeds you the Word of God, you are ready to fill others in your nation and other nations with the gospel of Jesus Christ. Ephesians 5:8-10 says, "For you were once darkness, but now you are light in the Lord. Walk as a child of light. For the fruit of the Spirit is in all goodness, righteousness, and truth, finding out what is acceptable to the Lord." Now that you know you walk in the Spirit, use the armor that God has placed in your heart that protects your fruit of the Spirit and your faith. In Ephesians 6: 11-20, the protection God has given you are: 1. Truth- a belt to guard your words; 2. Righteousness- a breastplate to protect your mind, will, and emotions; 3. Gospel of peace- a pair of shoes to walk by faith and hope and love; 4. Faith- the shield in your hand to protect your heart from evil works; 5. The Word of God- the Bible is a sword to cut down lies, deceit, tricks; 6. Salvation- a helmet that protects your belief and faith in Jesus Christ. God is Almighty, knowing that the evil power in the earth is trying to deceive you into unbelief, fear, guilt, and shame. God has given you power and authority over the devil, knowing you have a fleshly body that decays, full of dirt from the air you breathe and the people who are deceived. Therefore, you have to be led by God in all things so you can let go and let God show up to allow you to use your armor in every situation on every mind and body attack from the devil. God lets you know that you are set up to put up your guards and perform in a godly way. God wants you to show your Jesus walk, your Jesus talk, and your Jesus thoughts. "For we do not wrestle against flesh and blood, but against principalities, against little powers, against the rulers of darkness of this age, against spiritual hosts of wickedness in the heavenly places." (Ephesians 6:12) Believe that God has given you dominion over every evil way that confronts you every day of your life. God knows that your flesh is full of foul decay, a weight that you have to carry. He is your Creator and He alone is your faith, the center of your life. Jesus says, "I am the way, the truth, and the life." He is your light of life, your eternal life. You wear a body that is corrupting daily but, God will return to give you a body that will never corrupt. God is the same One who made heaven and earth. He will soon return to change all of His followers to immortal bodies to live in heaven. Depend on Jesus to carry you through this life where others will be attacked just to attack you and vice versa. You will sin because your mortal body is sin, dying daily. Hold on to the faith that has been delivered to you. Be strong to stand with the weapons God has provided so you fight to the end in these evil days. Without faith it is impossible to please God. "Go therefore, and make disciples of all nations, baptizing them in the name of the Father and of the Son and of the Holy Spirit." Thank God for His grace and truth that gives you faith to run this race for eternal life in Christ Jesus. Amen.

Forgiveness

"Be kind to one another, tenderhearted, forgiving one another, even as God in Christ has forgiven you." Ephesians 4:32 NLT

FATHER, SON AND Holy Ghost of Heaven, earth, and earth's undercoat, we praise You to the utmost! Open Your heavens and reveal Your Grace. Father let Your glory shine in our face! Father, Your Grace s a us forgive others as You have forgiven us, Your mercy is required of us, to do kindness with a tenderheart. Lord God, we love You first because You first loved us. We love You first because You created us. We live in Your image, Your image of salvation and deliverance. Father, we are here to show others Your love, not a hindrance. So. Let us pray to be kind, gentle, and giving; giving back love to those who trespass against us. O God hear our cry, we need Your answers to heal those in need of prayer. We need Your power to work in us as we show favor to the weak, favor to become fair. If we refuse to forgive others, O Father, these are the acts You will remember. If we confess to You, Lord, our sins, You are faithful and just to forgive us our sins and to cleanse us from all unrighteousness!" 1 John1:9 Your word says You will not forgive us if we refuse to forgive others since we are Your members full of Grace and truth, not rebellion. Forgiveness is a gift from You, Lord, we find in our hearts. It is not by might nor by power to forgive, but by Your Spirit, says the Lord God! Lord, we pray that forgiveness is renewed from faith to faith. We pray without ceasing, to forgive, to let go every weight! Your blood Jesus, was shed at Calvary as a living sacrifice. Our blood, Jesus, is cleansed through Your word, Your Holy Spirit, and our Savior Jesus Christ! Forgiveness, meaning the remission of sins, brings salvation and healing, Amen. Our great commission, meaning we go into all nations preaching the gospel, brings forgiveness in all hearts by God and by men. O Lord, Bless Your Holy Name.

Our Prayer to You, precious Lord, is a cry for the lost in all nations to hear this word, "The time is fulfilled, and the Kingdom of God is at hand. Repent, and believe in the gospel". Amen. (Mark2:15 NKJV) Lord, we pray that Your word keeps us in Your forgiving plan to win souls; that Your Holy Spirit inside of us keeps us from judging others who wrongfully treat us; and that the blood of Jesus keeps us giving love, peace, joy, kindness, faithfulness, gentleness, longsuffering, goodness and mercy with self control, in the name of Jesus! Father God, our prayer continually is to cry out to one another, "Your sins are forgiven, in Jesus name, Amen!" We stand on Your Word, Father God. You intercede for us saying, " I am in them and Father, You are in Me. May they experience such perfect unity that the world will know that You sent Me and that You love them as much as You love Me!" John 17:23. Father, now is the time for us to put You first in all we say and do. Father, we pray for You to search all the deep things of God. "Let no corrupt word proceed out of our mouths, but what is good for necessary edification, that it may impart Grace to the hearers. And do no grieve the Holy Spirit of God, by whom you were sealed for the day of redemption." Ephesians 4:29-30 NKJV Lord, show us the spiritual things we need to forgive, things in our hearts to let go, things in our mind to be transformed by the renewing process, and the spiritual things in our souls that may be strongholds needing the power of forgiveness, in Jesus name. Amen and Amen.

Godliness

And without controversy, great is the mystery of godliness: Christ was revealed in a human body and vindicated by the Spirit. He was seen by angels and announced to the nations. He was believed in throughout the world and taken to heaven in glory." 1 Timothy 3:16 NLT

IN THE NAME of Jesus Christ we come to the throne of Grace. Father God we know You as our first love, our first healer, and our only salvation. We bless You Lord, bless Your Holy Name. Father, we thank You for godliness, the instructions from the word of God to follow as obedient children. Amen. We thank You Father, for Your Holy Spirit inside of us giving us greater Grace and truth to manage our life. What a Mighty, Mighty God we serve! Hallelujah! Thank You, Jesus! We surrender our hearts to You, Jesus! "Bless the Lord O my soul and all that is within me, bless Your Holy Name!" Lord, hear our cry in this prayer for better godliness. We worship You Lord all the day long in prayer and supplication. "We are not ashamed of the gospel of Jesus Christ, for it is the power of God to salvation for everyone who believes, for the New first and also, for the Greek!" Romans 1:16 Our Prayer for holiness and righteousness is the same prayer from our hearts to receive godliness. Lord God. We come to You, Father, to know You and the power of Your might, to have the mind of Christ. Let God arise and His enemies be scattered! You said, Lord, in 1 John 3:2 these words to us, "Beloved, if our hearts do not condemn us, We have confidence toward God!" Thank You "Father for strength to know that we know! "If God the Father be for us,. You are more than the whole world against us. Amen. Father. Teach us thine will be done on earth as You have done in heaven! Let us be that light to set the captive free from the hands of the enemy!, Teach us to know the things of God, such as Acts 2:38, "Repent everyone of you and be baptized in the name of Jesus, for the remission of your sins, and you shall receive the gift of the Holy Spirit." Amen. You, "Lord, have given us, Your body, the Keys to the Kingdom of Heaven and whatever we bind on earth, will be bound in heaven. Whatever we loose on earth, will be loosed in heaven." Matthew 16:19 You are the Creator, Lord, who knows our beginning and our eternal end. All power and glory is in Your hands forever and ever as the Master of godliness on earth! Amen. "We thank You Lord of Heaven and earth, that You have hidden these things of godliness from the wise and prudent and have revealed them to babes..." Father, You have revealed these things to us through Your Holy Spirit. We pray Father that we reveal Your glory as we say and display whatever things that are pure, that are just, that are true and honest, lovely and of good report. Let these things be revealed in the name of Jesus, for holiness is next to godliness. Amen and Amen.

Judgement

"For with what judgement you judge, you will be judged; and with the measure you use, it will be measured back to you."
Matthew 7:2

WITH ALL HEARTS and minds on Jesus, Father we come before You thanking You for another day of blessings and great expectations. Lord, You said if we keep our minds stayed on You, You will keep us in perfect peace. Father , You are the Supreme judge. "For with what judgement you judge, you will be judged…" Father God we pray today that we cleanse from being judgemental to others knowing, Lord, that You will have to judge us the same way. There is now no condemnation to us who are in Christ Jesus, who walk not after the flesh but after the Spirit. Let Your will be known as we seek Christ as our own! Jesus, You spoke to blind men, saying, "Receive your sight!" Speak to us today, Lord, as we cry out for help! Jesus, our Lord and Savior, what are You saying to us? "Let not your heart be troubled: you believe in God, believe also in Me." Lord we need Your guidance as our Judge on earth as You are in heaven. Thank You, Lord for leading us, Your humble children, in doing right, teaching us Your ways. Father God, You are the Holy Spirit, and wherever the Spirit of the Lord is, there is freedom. Amen. You said in 1 Corinthians chapter eight, "But we must be careful so that our freedom does not cause others with a weaker conscience to stumble." Father God we pray today for those who are weak that You will increase their strength as we forgive those who trespass against us. Father God we understand we have to forgive others or You will not forgive us. You say in Your word, 1 Corinthians 11:31, "But if we would examine ourselves, we would not be judged by You, God, in this way." Father, we praise You for revealing how our forgiving others keeps us from Your judgement. "If we confess our sins, Lord, You are faithful and just to forgive us our sins and to cleanse us from all unrighteousness." 1 John 1:9. Father God, we pray today in Your word from Micah 6:8, "And this is what You require of us: to do what is right, to love mercy, and to walk humbly with You, our God." Father, You have commanded us to follow You with all our heart, all our soul, and all our mind. You have commanded us to love others as we love ourselves. Thank You, Jesus, for Your scripture telling us that we will be judged by what we are using to find fault in others. You teach us Father that You will also use that same measure on us that we are using to condemn others. "...And with the measure you use, it will be measured back to you." So Father God, now is the time for us to cast out what we wrestle against in these last and evil days. We pray for better decisions toward people since we wrestle not with flesh and blood. Lord, open our eyes to see that we have to cast down everything against the knowledge of God in the spiritual world. Amen. Let us continue to pray for the salvation of the lost, the forsaken, and our enemies to come to Jesus while they have time. "The day is near when You, Father God, will judge all godless nations...all their evil deeds will fall back on their own heads!" Lord, 6we know You will deliver us from every evil attack if we keep our minds stayed on You. You promise to keep us and bring us safely into Your heavenly Kingdom. All glory to God forever and ever. 2 Corinthians 5:10 we speak as we wait for the crown of righteousness in heaven, For we must all stand before Christ to be judged. We will each receive whatever we deserve for the good or evil we have done in this earthly body." We praise

You Jesus, Master of the universe. We bless Your Holy Name. "Now to You, Lord, who is able to keep us from falling, and to present us faultless before the presence of Your glory with exceeding joy! To the only wise God our Savior, be glory and majesty, dominion and power, both now and forever. In the name of Jesus we pray, Amen and Amen.

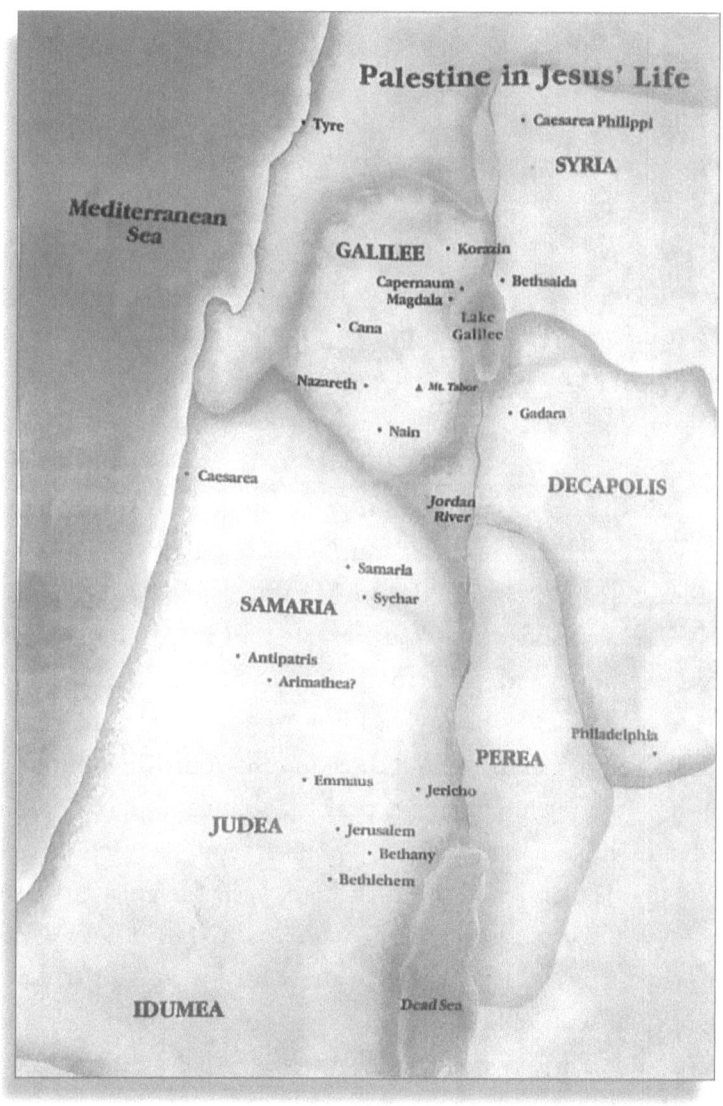

Kingdom Building

"And He said to them, 'Go into all the world and preach the gospel to every creature. He who believes and is baptized will be saved; but he who does not believe will be condemned. And these signs will follow those who believe. In My name they will cast out demons; they will speak with new tongues; they will take up serpents; and if they drink anything deadly, it will by no means hurt them; they will lay hands on the sick, and they will recover.'"
Mark16:15-18

ALL GLORY AND honor is to You, our Father in heaven. You are the great "I Am"! We stand in the midst of Your presence today with great joy and edification! You are Amazing! You are Marvelous! How Excellent is Your name! We rejoice and praise You for Life and Life more abundantly! Lord, we join hearts and hands for Your heavenly flow over the building not made by hands. Father, we ask for Your word to lead and guide Your vessels as we seek truth and direction for Your Kingdom on earth to be as it is in heaven. Father, we pray for abundance in the joining of the body of Christ in every nation. We know You have sent us to bring a harvest that is plentiful. Join us O Lord, Your servants, as we set sail to unknown places and preach the word to unknown faces. Send us, Jesus to the highways and hedges to draw the lost to Christ. Lord, let the mystery of. Christ be revealed. Our hope is built on nothing less than Jesus blood and righteousness! Amen. Father, we pray for a great anointing in Your people to prosper and be in good health even as our souls prosper in the Lord. Father, we yearn to earn Faith, greater Faith that is better than we've had before. Everyday with You, Jesus, is sweeter than the day before! What shall we do, Lord? Let us repent of our sins, our distractions and emotional reactions of things happening in this world. Father, You have changed us and we continue to repent of our sins and turn to You, for the Kingdom of Heaven is near! Father, what will we preach? Like 24:46 are the words You have spoken for Kingdom building. "Then Jesus, You said to them, "This it is written and thus it was necessary for the Christ to suffer and to rise from the dead the third day; and that repentance and remission of sins should be preached in His name to all nations, beginning at Jerusalem. And you are witnesses of these things. Behold, I send the Promise of My Father upon you; but tarry in the city of Jerusalem until you are endued with power from on high." There is power, power, wonder working power in the Blood of the Lamb! Father, You have spoken and Your children will do wonders to establish a firm foundation like the prophets of old. Let every word be gracious and true. God has spoken for us to agree. Amen! Jesu, we know You are Holy Spirit and Your Kingdom is in Spirit and Truth! Let this church agree. Amen! Galatians 6:8 settles Your word, "But those who live to please the Spirit will harvest everlasting life from the Spirit!" Father, we praise Your name as You live in us and walk with us through every ministry we are sent to do! You have purchased us with a high price to love better than the world, live better than the world, and lighten up in our hearts, minds, and souls better than the world! All things are possible to us who believe! Thank You, Lord for life, health, and strength to build Your Kingdom! Right now, Lord, we receive the power of the Holy Spirit giving us Your abundance, Your increase, so we will be better missionaries going into all nations. We are Your witnesses of so great a faith, telling people about the Christ everywhere from now until Your rerun to earth. Father, let the words of our mouths and the meditations of our hearts be acceptable in Your sight, O Lord our strength and Redeemed! In Jesus name we pray, Amen and Amen.

Liberty

"This is the new covenant I will make with My people on that day, says the Lord. I will put My laws in their hearts, and I will write them on their minds. I will never remember their sins and lawless deeds." Hebrews 10:16-17 NLT

Worship Service at Highway Christian Church

WE COME BEFORE You, Lord Jesus, thanking You for Your saving grace! Father God, You created us for such a time as this, You created heaven and earth for Your praises. Praise the Lord with gladness! We come before You, Lord, with joy unspeakable and full of glory! We give You all the honor, all the glory, and all the praise now and forevermore! Today, Father we bless You for liberty in Jesus name! Hallelujah! Father, You are able and willing to set us free from sickness, free from disease, free from hatred, free from shame! O Lord our God! We cry out for healing and deliverance today! Set us free Lord from anything causing harm to Your Spirit, Lord! Deliver us from every weight that So easily beset us! Father You said where the Spirit of the Lord is there is liberty! Thank You Father for being faithful to Your word! We are here today because of the Liberty we have. It is a gift from You, God. "For God presented Jesus as the sacrifice for sin. People are made right with God when they believe that Jesus sacrificed His life, shedding His blood." Romans 3:25 "He whom the Son has set free, is free indeed!" We bless the new covenant of faith. Our new covenant of hope in eternal life. We bless our new covenant of love, full of Grace and truth. "For you brethren, have been called to liberty, only do not use liberty as an opportunity for the flesh, But through love serve one another." Galatians 5:13 Your goodness and mercy endures forever through Your covenant. We can come before You believing that our hearts are cleansed by Your blood. Father God, we stand in Your presence as a child of God, forgiven of all our sins and set free by Your love. "For God so loved the world that He gave His only begotten Son, that whosoever believes in Him will not perish, But have everlasting life." Thank You, Lord for life eternal that You have promised to those who believe. Lord, we have an agreement together, a covenant, that we promise to keep because You have written Your words in our hearts and planted truth and Grace in our minds! Lord, Lord, Hallelujah! We agree to speak Your words that You have placed in our hearts. Father, we will keep our covenant with You, giving back to You by serving You, Lord! Let us commit ourselves to Your service, having the mind of Christ! Amen. Liberty is obedience to Your will, Lord. Liberty is freedom to speak love and giving love, justice, and mercy to all people. God is love! Amen. Our Prayer today and everyday, Lord, is to trust And believe. Our faith makes us whole. We bless You Lord for washing away our sins and lawlessness! "For we did not receive the Spirit of bondage again to fear, but we received the Spirit of adoption by whom we cry out, 'Abba, Father.'" Romans 8:15 Liberty is the blood of Jesus that cleanses us, it leads us into the path of righteousness, and sets us free from all unrighteousness, in Jesus name. Bless You Lord forever and we will speak Your truths. Your words have we hid in our hearts that we may not sin against You. Father, You said You will remember Your covenant of life eternal and liberty, Your covenant of love that You commanded for one thousand generations. Father, Your words will forever live in Your people, in Jesus name we pray, Amen and Amen.

Miracles

"If I will not open for you the Windows of Heaven and pour for you such blessing that there will not be room enough to receive it. And I will rebuke the devoured for Your sakes so that he will not destroy the fruit of Your ground nor shall the vine fail to bear fruit for you in the field, says the Lord of hosts. And all nations will call you blessed for you will be a delightful land, says the Lord of hosts." Malachi 3:10-11

O LORD, OUR God in heaven above. We come before You as Your humble servants! Shine on us today. Show Your glory as we give You all the honor and praise! To God be the glory! Hallelujah! Hallelujah! Hallelujah! Praise Your name! We Thank You Father for this day and every day of new mercies! We bless You Lord for our waking up this morning and our life, health and strength. If it had not been for the Lord on my side, where would I be, oh Lord where would I be! The heavens proclaim Your glory and the earth is Yours and the fullness thereof. Touch this prayer meeting that Your glory will be revealed. Where two or three are gathered together in the name of Jesus, Lord we see You in the midst of us. You said in Your word, "Again I say to you that if two of you agree on earth concerning anything that you ask, it will be done for you, by My Father in heaven! Amen. We pray for miracles today as we touch and agree in the name of Jesus! Lord, God open Your healing virtue on every soul on our prayer list! We cry out, Abba! Father of Heaven and earth, rest in the hearts and bodies of

Your people. Take away every sickness and every disease, every burden and every pain in the souls of these people on the altar, in the name of Jesus! Lord, You say whatever we bind on earth, will b e bound in h raven! Whatever we loose o n earth, will be loosed in heaven, in the name of Jesus! Lord, we bind the demons of financial stress, physical stress, and mental stress and release clear minds, supply of money to meet every need in the name of Jesus. Father, we cast down every imagination against the knowledge of Jesus. You say Father, if we believe, we can speak to that mountain of stress and mental unrest, any mountain in our lives to be moved and cast out into the sea and it will be done, in Jesus name! Father a God through the Holy Spirit in us, We trust and believe that miracles are done in every soul right now in the name of Jesus. We rebuke the devourer in the name of Jesus! Hallelujah! Hallelujah! We call miracles done, healing is done! It is well in our souls, in Jesus name! We are blessed in every avenue of our bodies and every desire for the Lord in our hearts, in Jesus name! Amen and Amen.

Upward Bound

"Since you have been raised to new life with Christ, set your sights on the realities of Heaven, where Christ sits in the place of honor at God's right hand. Think about the things of Heaven, not the things of earth. For you died to this life, and your real life is hidden with Christ in God." Colossians 3:1-3 NLT

Heaven

REJOICE IN THE Lord always, and again I say, Rejoice! We give honor to God as we come before You in prayer and thanksgiving! Father God, the author and finisher of our faith, we thank and praise You for all You've done. When I think of the goodness of Jesus and all He's done for me, my soul cries out Hallelujah! Praise God for saving me! Hallelujah! We Come before You, Lord with praise and worship! Thank You, Lord for this day, for this is the day the Lord has made and we will rejoice and be glad in it! Hallelujah! We rejoice in knowing that We are washed in Your blood Jesus. We are free from the cares of this world, Lord, when we depend on You! Jesus, We hear You saying, "Come to Me all You who labor and are heavy laden and I will give you rest. Take My yoke upon you and learn from Me, for I am gentle and lowly in heart, and you will find that for your souls." Lord, let us rest from our burdens as we come today to praise and glorify Your name! We walk by faith in You, Jesus! Father, we loose all our guilt and shame as we look upward for a better future! Lord, You promised us eternal life in Christ in a place You have prepared for us! Precious Lord, lead us today and every day to that rock that is higher than this earth. Our Father who art in heaven, hallowed be Your name. Your Kingdom come! Your will be done on earth as it is in heaven! Amen. Lord Your word says, "Heaven is My throne, and the earth is My footstool!" Isaiah 66:1 We bless Your Holy Name forever and ever as we speak Your word, "Remember the Lord will give us an inheritance as our reward, and that the Master We are serving is Christ!" We are bound for heaven, our home. "For all creation is waiting eagerly for that future day when You, God will reveal who Your children really are…including the new bodies You have promised us." Lord, let the words of our mouths and the meditations of our hearts be about heavenly things, about our death with Christ and our newness of life. "For we know that if our earthly house, this tent, is destroyed, we have a building from God, a house not made with hands, eternal in the heavens." 2 Corinthians 5:1 Holy Spirit we bless You as we serve the Lord with gladness. Thank You Father for our upward bound future. Your eternal word and eternal Spirit stands firm in heaven. Glory to God in the highest! Peace on earth and goodwill to all men. In Jesus name we pray, Amen and Amen.

CHILD OF THE KING
By Mary Bethea

Sing to tune of "I Thank You, Jesus! I Thank You, Lord"

When I was a child, Lord,
I spoke as a child!
I understood You were watching…
watching over me.
Now that I know, Lord,
You're the light of the world,
I'm going to show Your ways, Lord,
what's acceptable to You.

Change my thoughts, Lord,
And my childish ways!
I'm putting them away, Lord,
You have set me free!
Free to live for Jesus!
My light and my salvation,
I thank you for your love, Lord,
I'm a child of the King.

Walking in the light, Lord!
Your Beau...tiful light!
It's where a child of the King shines,
By day and by night!
Here to glorify Jesus,
Filled with Your Holy Spirit,
I thank You for Your grace, Lord,
I'm a child of the King.

I praise You Jesus!
My Bless-sed Savior,
For all the great things, Lord!
You've done for me.
How You baptized me, Lord!
In the name of Jesus!
You gave me the mind of Christ!
I'm a child of the King.